POLYNOMIALS AND POLLEN

Polyno mials

and

Pollen

PARABLES, PROVERBS,

PARADIGMS, AND

PRAISE FOR LOIS

Jay Wright

DALKEY ARCHIVE PRESS

CHAMPAIGN & LONDON

The author wishes to thank the editors of
the following journals, in which some
of these poems were previously published:
Chelsea, *Mandorla*, *Michigan Quarterly Review*,
Nocturnes, and *The Southern Review*.

Library of Congress Cataloging-in-Publication Data
Wright, Jay, 1934–
Polynomials and pollen : parables, proverbs, paradigms
and praise for Lois / Jay Wright. — 1st ed.
p. cm.
ISBN-13: 978-1-56478-499-5 (acid-free paper)
ISBN-10: 1-56478-499-1 (acid-free paper)
I. Title.
PS3573.R5364P65 2008
811'.54—dc22
2007042156

Partially funded by a grant from the Illinois
Arts Council, a state agency, and by the
University of Illinois, Urbana-Champaign

www.dalkeyarchive.com

Designed and composed by Quemadura
Printed on permanent/durable
acid-free, recycled paper, and bound
in the United States of America

ONE / IMÙLẸ̀

The fothergilla major
      becomes
         an acceptable
            device for spring.
The poet
    measures his anxiety
        in the glabrous leaf,
or the conspicuous white of May.
So much is a dream
      of orange yellow autumn
            mountains,
so much is the inconspicuous
nerve rending of solitude
where the garden begins, or ends
    —the shrub teaching
        the exhilaration of retreat,
perhaps a rest,
   perhaps the deciduous
      invention of time.
One must carefully walk
    these paths,
for the color burns,
and the acid underfoot

commemorates
an ethereal disappearance.
Nothing speaks easily—
          of possession
or of the authentic river
and that special case,
that indeterminate event
beyond the light of darkness.
So the shrub awakens
          a spontaneous proof
          of kinship in moist
soil, shadows and sun,
and every resolution
          can only be true
                    or false.

The light blue apple
  imposes its will
    upon this sentence.
That discrete linear ordering
  becomes the possible
    existence,
the grammar's prankster,
the liberated evidence
    of a necessary sacrifice.

If coral could speak to me,
my gift would be forgiven.
Take this as a cunning
state of affairs,
whatever is made possible
                by grace alone,
say, that suffering
occasioned by exhilaration,
a corrupted intention
                that does not fit.
Why should I bother
to match the great order of nature,
or feel compelled
to live
in the geometric
contradiction some lily intends?
There is a moment
when that brief red motion
leaves the deep water
                for air.

Old enough to remember
the river girdled by sand,
I know that the shadow
that falls between speech
                and fact

is wholly rational.

Clever figures lie in wait
for the innocent weaver
                of the soul's cloth.
If they were worms,
they would divest her.
One must speak sweetly of ambrosial
springs, those palpable
endeavors cued by a syntax
                akin to the dead.
I remind you of the hymnal
exigencies of the exalted vessel,
and the sound the Zany Denim
                would easily capture.
I hope to flow broadside to the current,
and become a standing pool
or a meritorious stream.
These architectural conundra
sing brotós, blood brooking daring
that offers no solace.
But you will recall the celtic clamor
that attributed much
                to the enterprise
and most corrupting exchange
                of going naked.

Impatiently stable,
the granite escapes
            a spectrum of
                its own de-
                    sign.
Heat will tell, or prose it
differently, the fabled
                energeia
                    leaves its bed
to wed and bear witness
to that improvised
            vehicular
                event that
                    spells its
                        name.
Ice,
or wind,
or water,
driven, faded
force becomes the voice
one hears at the summit.

The ruby of Rio Lerma
                compels us still,
or that will of stillness,
the word broken,
if unintended, or an
intention of an angel's
                thoroughfare.
And nowhere
will the habitation we required
recall our presence.
If someone asks
the density of absent water,
we, standing on Rio Lerma,
will know surely
                she is mistaken.
Yet there must be fools like us,
measuring the hue and pitch
                of the founding stone.

Now,
at the end of day
Democritus shakes his clever head,
and wonders,
        how could such darkness
fall upon a desert
lit by his meditation,
strutted by his archaic
                imagination?
This is south of everywhere,
a map of meanderings
in which the morning sun
        feels an intrusion.
I began this arrangement
to tell you
how I had threaded my way
from the Great Basin
        to stand, eye to eye,
with the Vermilion flycatcher,
and had come to understand
        my skin's vermilion cast.
But I am easily distracted
from devastation,

and every note that reminds me of loss.
Shaggy Democritus appeals to me,
with his wanderlust,
and his eye, attuned to meteors
and eclipses, fishes and whirlwinds,
with his estrangement
from Athens

        and his own passion.
Nothing happens by chance,
not even the inevitable shipwreck
of love's recognition,
and the spiraling disturbance
in the bones of a star.
The savannah insistence I bring
to my being is a heavy storm,
involved

        in the ferrying water
of my constantly changing
                breath.

II^7V^7

This sound
will submit to its first fall,
to the edgy ground
prepared by silence. That mark
soon masks
a most engaging recall
and perfect bridging
tremor of a false tuning.

Such round
certitude uncovers all
that one might have found
with a patient ear. Why think
the taut
resolution a pitfall?
Why stumble through four
phases of a song gone sour?

Will this
attentive indirection

appear an abyss,
a token gallimaufry,
galling
spit, subject to correction?
Or will such constant
motion contest its descent?

Profound
fallacy, time breeds a small
notion to propound
an instrumental pulsing,
the pause
that courts the wish to install
itself as the thread
and perfect measure of trust.

Baldomero
tied these infant leaves
to the wind.

                  By grace,
he removed their fear.
What does it matter
that the aspen mind
        remains a token,
or a misconception
in the umbilical behavior
        of dust and gas?
Surely,
under these dusted stars at Jemez
one might conceive resonant
misgivings,
or a lunar power
that has assembled a cave
        of talkative birds.
Whatever walks wayward
over the starchy red clay
        compels a thief's ambition.
We are light years
beyond the green brushstroke

of that island
and the orienting
distemper of its solitude.
It would be comforting
to sit in state with the unnameable
monuments of death,
as alert as Jabès to their treason.
Only the fragmented
festivity of golden cups
        might concern us,
and singing alone would be
our portion.
                But you
are capable of hemlock's presence
and the far-shining fire
        of the simple appearance
                of love.

I have been given
the occasion of your name,
though what is actual, perhaps,
                    escapes.
Better to speak quickly
of such disappearances
        and to evade that donnish
dance around existence.
Someone we know
stands weaving the charitable
trust scrolled by the past,
and has been too forgiving
        in the matter of a shaping
        ens.
I will insist
upon my body's endurable grammar
even as the world grows silent,
or gives in to a creative
                    forgetfulness.
And there must be a line of sparrows
who have broken
            the code of your name.

Someone will say
we secretly composed elegiac verses,
and came in person
                    to sing them
for the familiar death of a stranger.
Not lovely Mixcoac,
not gracious Coyoacán
could arrest the word owed
                    to destruction.
We have given ourselves
to the art of threading remorse
for beauty.
            No one welcomes us;
no one wishes we were gone.
On Isabel la Católica,
the amber insistence of night
lights a flinty space
            to celebrate a life's
                    fulfillment.
And we are singers
            trained at Salamis.

I would speak of the improbability
of incarnation, the natural
            body on the wing,
the self-restraint circuitously
displayed, the salvaged
            substance become
a meridian, a parallel,
            that passion called suffering.
Discretion turns me reticent.
Lately, I have been adept
at misreading my body's
            stance, the chance verdict
the sullen trickster records
where death will not go.
            Let no one mistake
the expedient origin
            of uplifted moments
                  for an unbreakable order.

Praise
the making of waters.
All praise
to the transparent universe,
the small contamination
                    of matter.
If these are words
not my own,
                    I remain
grateful
        for such concern
        with the dead.
Thus,
if I had a fillet of fine wool,
a winged new hymn,
an archaic passion
for everflowing rivers,
            and knew myself
            a symbolic process,
I could account
for the consummate name.
Perhaps that is the trace of absence,
the frugal insistence I hear

in eternity,
in the speculative moment
when memory has no role to play,
and the aten sheds the sand,
and comes streaming to my eye.
How competent is that fiction?
How able is the body to count
its figments and filigrees
as fact?
Like a wind falling on oaks
on a mountain,
a certain resignation
came to me,
and filled me with the tumult
of waters that refused
the ingenuity of clocks,
the disingenuousness of the rustic
shores that fade.
Count me as another
burnt by the elemental passion
of waters,
embraced by an irretrievable
word.

TWO / SASA

Egregiously atomic
anger sits on its flaccid stool
and watches me.
                A fixed star
has dropped its pail
into the thorough silence.
Whatever was branching dust
now shows itself immune
             to my urging,
the last gift
    of a disencumbrance
love will not allow.
Singular, salutary friend,
I wear my little felt cap
             to celebrate
an indefensible sleep.
Late now, that fledging body
scurries to its shelter.

The youngest among us
know grief, and grief enough.
We who linger
dedicate ourselves
                to amorphous change,
something we seem to have
learned from an epigram
                on a Phrygian tomb.
The youngest among us
think that I surpass
many in honor,
and cast my javelin
too near forbidden ground.
But I am dedicated
to the young, the banquet
        and the frightful aulos
that welcomes what we
        had forbidden to appear.

That poet told us
even friends would betray those who have died.
So there is no shame
in forgetting the translation
of these streets,
or the evenings we spent
constructing a bird that would fly
bravely at dawn.
There is no matter to the matter-
at-hand that leaves us intact,
expressible and weary
        from our own regard,
nothing to concern us
in the steaming cebollas
        fogging a taco cart.

How delightful
        the displacement
            of the purple finch;
only an otherwise
        could be wise enough
            to sustain
                its distress.

What could
        our turbulent lexicon,
served, if not provoked,
by the inventive tamarisk,
submit to the experimental
constraint,
the freistimmig displacement
        of a feathery voice
            that has gone out of tune?

Every woven robe begins
a counter sound, eight steps perhaps
above the range of my proper
voice, that sound caught flat by measure,
a displaced entrance given no
time to prepare or to thread its
presence near the conjugal weight
of bells. Certainly, such music
lives without the divinity
of form or astringent purpose
in civil disobedience.
One ought to keep to the measure
of redemptive scales and altered
themes, and feel the tempered ascent
disfigure the hand, and the mind,
and see the tonic fabric fall
to rest, and resting, wed itself
to gesture and dissolution.

Coffin click
of the wasted hour.
What would you give if not
the sanction you disapprove?
speaking of return there where
the counterpoint of breath
contrary to its use
consumes you,
or stated
otherwise becomes
a necessary stream,
or the point incidental
to its trace,
the light its only
intention, steered or stewed
by this moment's breviary?

I am two fools I know,
for naming and for saying no
to the Damascene folly,
my soul's extent and nature
neverwhere more Solomonic
and extemporaneously sure,
if bemusement would befriend
or thoroughly upend
this testamental solitude
everywhere a certitude
that denies the pressure
and magmatic flow, say glow,
the intentional content, know
of my state of affairs—
I say two, and Damascene,
                    and no.

I shall wear
the dying bull's eroticism
when sunset provokes
                me to speech,
and shall be attendant
to love's furry delirium
at night's propulsive end.
You cannot ask me
how the Spanish vowel
has coiled around my song
and made it difficult
                to sow.

This book wants to ride
its hands to another stop.
                    Why stop?
Why go on?
Why fill the cardinal's
            poplar with rain,
or the strain of its cleaving?
The thorough green
lies brown on the beech.
Every signature of presence
            has been correlated
                with the fleshy desire
of the map we left behind.
Who will quarrel
        with the lexicon of need?

Good morning, cornbread.
Here's your heartache of beans
and gruel,
                    tempered figment,
a blessing,
                    a fallible
consistency
                    appended
                    to angel breath.
Now that is a leavened
undertaking you refused
                    to consider.

Such is the note at Harvard,
a native pitch and blackguard
insinuation of rhyme.
Who would go reeling for prime
dissonances and display,
or believe not that the lay
chorale and crude cultured stone
these voices offer in their bone
bred fragility could lead
straight to an improvised need
no one could endure, or speak,
or ruin in a fit of pique?

Forty days should be enough
to string the rosaceous
            temporall blather
the dour dean brought
            to Santa Rosa.
Neglectful of roses, that fellow.
An Irishman by report,
enamored of Indians and fleet
                  mulattoes.
Well, none of this will play
when the altar gets established
in Santa Fe,
            and the sly Murphys
try to derive a Corcoran
                  from Cork
and a mulish poet spreads
his sour phlogiston
            over Jersey.

Every city invites
        a purging rain,
and along the way the plain
chant of waters
        that have been sheltered
            by an attendant willow.
Initiates come bounding,
        beyond their arbitrary
            dangers and desires,
in search of the triste
        panoply, dry
            and unforgiving,
of parallel rivers
        on their way to a death.
Such is the way of rain.
One cannot speak
        too sharply of cities.

New folk clamber
up the cloudscape
    of etymological intention,
turn left at semantic difficulty
and burrow into the bushbound hole
    (unusual for clouds)
    of tattered semes.
The sentential sentences
that started us on our way
    have long ago abandoned us.
Who can spell
    the swelling paraplasm
      that announces
        a new direction?
Circumventing my circumplex,
I need to invent a reason
    to address the circumferential
status of this lonely
      and lovely
        word
          here.

Age has given us a map
to affective ambition.
Or shall we call it affection,
or love,
            a peasant's stroll
through the lanterns
that remain along this way?
How can this city
ask us to return
when the very young speak
only to the greyest stones,
and the greyest among us
            boast of having never
                        arrived?
What river
bleeding from Bellas Artes
is wide enough
to carry us past the incense
and silk of memory?
As the day falls,
I lean into your hair,
and whisper
that I have seen a solitary
leaf
        where once there were trees.

Wednesday
would worry
the most intrepid soul.
Seven A.M. Teacups
and the plasticity of sleeplessness.
This down,
            if you set,
a morning bemused
by the raw presence
that greets you in Dundee,
carefully
            such confusion
of conversations
concerning caraway and cunning
improbabilities—

            a dory that cannot dock
            in this dream, and
            a memory of liquids
            and fricatives
given the pleasures place ensures.
All is a hallowed bushing,
undamaged, turbulent tongues.

In the vatic chamber
the cat sniffs
        a benevolent certitude,
a cellular indifference
                        to error,
not once but ever irregular
composition of a will
too immune to the fledging
                and structural
mesh of a body gone
                momentously dry.
Such is the way of creatures
at ease upon the spiny
ladder that stretches
                from moon to moon,
the etymology of chance
that makes sense of breath.

Serpent coils upon a wall
   engender eternity, or
    the shabby image
we might call our well-being.
I am treacherous
 to circular fire;
I make myself a lyre
  out of gaudy notions
   which lie
fringed with the sensation
   of self-betrayal.
One might hope
   for compassion
    in a linear
     benevolence
that disguises a troublesome
     note.

Over time,
the foot forgets the dance,
or the fiddler inhibits
the flux occasioned
by bone tethered density.
Wake to a process
               of induction,
a presupposing love
unsettled in our present state.
There *is* a theology concerned
with music,
and the science of difficult
beginnings
               in a curry
                    of astonished
                         aer.

THREE / BÓLÍ

Those who thoroughly bed
the estuary
            know
the value of relation,
the inflection and formal
variation
            water knows
                    from air.
Clearly,
everything consists
in the determinate word,
the order of one, two, three;
no tricky exclusion concerns us—
not here, not ever.
            Can I say I am
                    an island
where every moment submits
to an articulation
        of a banyan tree
        and Gaelic letter
        asleep
            on an ancient page?
These are canonical hours.

And this looks like the particle
syntax
           we have cudgeled into being.
At times like this,
you might hear the lyrical Khepera,
and see the frugal light
of another sun
           that articulates
                the river.
It is too soon to say
    if blindness
is the innocent gift
           of strangers.

What is holy
follows me where
a threadbare intonation
        (that flare and wellspring)
                no nothing indicts.
En kurioi,
it must be an affliction
that sits heavy on the ear.
I have taken a Paulish
entablature,
                call it, if you will,
a name
        to distribute
through the shaggy court.
My nave and navel
sympathies betray
an inventive solitude,
        but there
you have me croned
by fallacious fervor
                and fraught
with a gift
        of faithful
                forgetting.

I would go, no,
over the ground,
        say once,
say again,
        if only
the perfect strangeness,
        called symmetry,
could be fiddled
                and fluted
into angels who
        had given me their word
and a fit engine
that never stalls
                at boundaries.

Donde huasteca,
Rogaciano,
            pero
this rhythm is subversive—
durable, yes,
                but unfathomable—
a sweetness that can't
get arrested in Tuc-son.
Do I know you?
Seguro, under los dos
arbolitos
            there waits
a wounded cicada,
and I am its companion,
a daybreak artist
            who keeps
a silver dollar vested
                close to the bone.
Such harmony lies
in a foolish investment
                called love.

No word in this
ferrous nativity
              plays as well
as blue-shadowed silk.
You notice
              the elaboration
                            of phrase
that misconstrual
              of number
and the cradled designation
that skirls about and betrays
   itself,
              when what is done
                            bears the flame
                            and fashion
that night rending deeds
intend
              in giving birth
                            to silk.

Someone will have to account
for the vermilion chair in the room,
where the heather green quilt
              and cream walls
have set their domain.
One hears
        the mathematical talk
              that makes sense
of an arrayable disjunction
and the flight
        into a Babylon
only the ghost knows.
Could it be that the smallest
bundle of light
        has a mind of its own,
or perhaps some paradoxical
and raffish frenzy
has found a home?

SIX ON SIX ON SIX: THE DILEMMA OF THE RAISED SIXTH

The modal logic
of aspiration leaves
me breathless—

all that equivalence
all that smudged
recursion, complete

contextual mesh,
fragile imaginings
setting what

is possible beside
the all too
necessary absence.

*

What is the evidence
for my pulse
a slow intrusion
of mountain, a bird's beak
in desert
onion, hemistich
of water filled with sand,
a curried
bush that clever stars
ignite and send away?
I need death
to figure the dance.

*

Suet soothes
the hairy woodpecker,
structures his hazy

world; thereby
the redcapped flicker
flies into an alder

to peck its
wounds, opens another
form of illusion,

a minor
intrusion that one might
again set afire.

*

The integrity
of polar air seems lost
in the soft

conjunction, the ontic
play, common
upheaval of fixed

and furry creatures
who pretend to be wed.
Never think

the petty confusion
admits a
parson's hoary tale.

*

How clumsy the syntax
of belief—
a slough of prunish

inversions—now appears;
if only
time's second arrow

were companionable,
or at least
receptively figured

in the shallow blue trace
that nothing
explains or removes.

*

What should you
say of the effective
construction of death,

that council
of determinate form
that implausibly

gathers your
breath and will faithfully
spiral it, weightless

and pointless,
toward the moment that gold
becomes imperfect?

=

Red is a difficult axiom,
  a culling insistence
      of fathers
who were blinded
              by starlight
and affected
          by carbonaceous
particles
          that taught them
          to dance.

This migratory red seems out of place.
I can see it fall near the root
of the ceiba tree, a studious space
that welcomes death, that filtered truth.
Perhaps this spin of sun begins the chase,
the particle flow of a boat
set on its shifting course. Where is the trace
of Tlaloc's domain? That fine cloth,
absolute loss, seems easy to embrace.
I go east and south, west and north,
provoked by silence, the commonplace
refusal to swear another oath
to the figure and ground of hidden grace.
I know the dusty labyrinth
of stars obscures me, threatens to erase
my body's bright archive, uproot
the scandalous order that is the case.
My being wanders the seventh
dimension of fertility, the base
of shifting ground and that rude
insistent darkness that makes loss love's face.
This migratory red is just
the night's desire for morning's thrilling pace.

Wednesday awakens its twin
where light goes.
                        This invitation
                            to speech
clarifies its coming,
a becoming indigenous
jewel of canyon strata.
Stand where the stand overlooks
        the spent shallow seas;
these have been covered with ease
by a gray redemptive intention.
And so I speak thus,
        a chronicler of shadows,
            or of winds that have
sunned themselves
        into a willful
                disappearance.

The clerk with the climate
in his pocket could stir
an anger that never recedes.
Let him attune himself
to the cumulus that keeps
          his morbid catch
                    at home.

Love is an economist,
tenaciously counting its gifts—
sea shells and polished stones—
on an abandoned beach.
Late, through the encumbered fog,
a ferrying innocence arrives
                    just in time.
Who, though, would have thought
such a sedulous banker
            would need the thin skills
                        of a junker
riding perilously low
in high water?
Oh, if only someone would
teach me how to praise
the weathered insignia
            of those who have survived
                        the gathering.

In that apparent country
reason does hard time.
Where is the evidence of solid
ground for the doubtful,
　　　doubting or doubtless
　　　　　fecundity,
that abyss and field of force,
the differential glimmering
　　　of a voiceless presence?
They come to us,
　　　these resilient travelers,
with words we cannot say, an
expressiveness
　　　determined
by a desire to pass
　　　from knowing
　　　　　to being.
Who now will anoint
them, and speak of them
as one would do
　　　when standing
on love's complementary
　　　　　estate?

I would be pleased
to deliver my book
            to the dead,
and submit
to the ingenious logic of graves.
Perhaps, I would be greeted
with an endurable
            circumspection,
or a cascade of promises
with an elementary charge.
We then could speak
of the shadow of wings,
a rejoicing
in the modulation in darkness
and the improbability of being
            in time.
Nothing in my book
tells of the deathwatch
      in a Buenos Aires barrio,
the fabled engagement
of a brutish singer
            with death,
the frail wisdom

imaged in a habit of books,
                    or a key.
If I—this evening—
were to travel South Broadway
in search of a silence
        that ornaments my world,
I would understand
the construction of a village,
the determinate dignity of the dead
and their suspicious
            parsing of an everflowing
                            river.

Romualdo would trade
the laurel
            for a double.
Did he know
the danger in violets?
They farmed him south
                for his bat.
He found himself
surrounded by a great forest
and bereft of his balche.
What could I tell him?
I, who had been too much engaged
with the authentic olive tree
and an impossible voice
        I thought its own reward.
This marks the end of our season,
fortuita cosa de tiempo,
            sand in an hourglass.

Nine miles from home,
near les chants populaires
de la Belle France,
I come upon myself,
serving whiskey to mourners
                    at my wake.
An egg sits at table,
and a brocade of budgies is at the door.
Why notice these things?
Don't I have enough to concern me
with the care and feeding of the bereft?
Someone tries to impress upon me
that there are rules
for these invocations, habits
that even the absent-minded
                    and ill-disposed
                        easily recall.
Did I, at the moment of my death,
place my hand on the proper urn,
and speak in a purple voice,
                    grainy with distance?
If not,
may I be forgiven the arrogance
of cinching my mortality to my waist.

FOUR / ILHUITL

I must tell you
        of the circular
            experience of chickadees,
and pipe the dogmatic
        array of their dipping
                            flight,
the way they betray
the lilac's late summer
                    stodginess,
when, out of morning's
        burnt phase,
they begin to phrase
        their imitative
and incendiary hymns.
Why speak of such necromancers?
Why give space
        in this ring of existence
                to fledgers
who will comb the morning
for able-bodied seed
        going and gone
                to dust?
These nunnish nitpickers

thread the air
        with their
indecipherable geometries,
fade and fit in a cherry basket,
with a beamish eye
        fixed on the nearest
                stranger.

Who will defend the raven,
      or the blackheaded jay,
      or be persuaded of the plover's
            indifference,
if there is no account
of the unbroken flow
      of a classical star
toward the moment
      it fades away?
These words lie bracken
upon my memory; other voices
      have framed them;
and the murmur of furry beings
turns my attention
      from the wounded cry
            of a disenchanted bird.

What bird did the Napolitano
have in mind?
Was it the cactus wren,
that crossbarred forager
      snuffling around
          the mesquite?
Góngora
undoubtedly never saw
aquel pajarillo que vuela
close to the rain,
one that had the figured
sign and sound of a distant
Akan voice,
          one given
to sleeping late
and awaking near the feather
of arid hills.
Borges awakened his amazed
and icy house
in the white light of a wasteful day
and heard his bird
      acclaiming the silence.
Certainly,

the silence of Buenos Aires
should be a provocation,
                    even here,
and the nesting complicity
of deserts on the rise
should engender a shame in me,
or a flaw,
or the arresting innocence
of thinking eternity
the absolute bird.
Such is the thermal
equilibrium of stars
            that I have forgotten
how easy it is
            to lose myself
in the flags and morcillas
            the night always displays.

Troubadours and mallards
love their ponds
        the mollusks
        and small fish
attendant there
and love as well
        the attendant confusion
when the surface breaks
and the watery velum
        turns antsy
          with figures
These are terribly muddled
          semblances
arch duplicities
astringent conjoinings
        an April choir's
filigreed benevolence
that will allow no one
        ni troubadour
        ni mallard
to sing bass

The redbud has elected
its constituents.

                 They gather
along the stone path
at the edge of the garden.
They flutter,
       they fall and rise;
       they know it is autumn,
       and there is an exacting
       warmth lying
              underfoot.
Whatever comforts them
escapes,
       and triggers
the election that explains
all that resolves
      the proper flow,
the properties that give themselves
to their disappearance.

I cannot abide
that spiky desert calico,
too bristly by half,
too sure of its perfect flower.
I deplore its devilish
attachment
                   to gravel,
the way it challenges March
and dares to breathe
near summer.
I will not celebrate
its tufted courage,
if, in doing so, I call
attention
to the rough edge
of a universe I have not
managed to tame.

God bless this skunky plant,
with its small blue flowers
and a name
                        that could
lead you down the wrong paths.
The little seeds can feed
hunger
                        or help to slake a thirst.
So the washes have learned
an exhibiting embrace.
The rainfall uncovers
a probable body that abides.
All's right in the family of mint,
even if this little villain
plays cat-and-mouse
                        with secret beings
in transit further south.

How ingenious of this
spring-fed pond
        to pipe its name
abroad—
        Quitobaquito,
an echo too close
to the sonorous
        pachanga of grifería.
Then again,
what would be gained
by drawing a nightshade,
nibbling at the mushrooming
green,
        and mumbling
about the danger of such
                radiance?
Further away,
there are gypsum dunes,
nude, prissy with a special
                silence.

Qui veut faire confession . . .
Next awry of my hand
I will set a unicorn,
something to disenchant
        the Canadian, or
brough up the Common-
wealth of me.
A folded text would be exact,
tactful,
perhaps as factual
        as the provincial
provenance
        these impertinent
linguists require.
                So here
I sit in Cambridge,
cadging drinks, snuffed
in tweeds,
        and trying
to pretend that I submit
to party discipline.
                What,
sir, is the argument? What,

sir, contorts your fuzzy mug?
I began with a wish
to be true to a spell
            that was cast
by an attention to unacceptable
tenses.
            Who says the flow
that exhausts a preterite
banquet needs to make sense?
Falcon,
            eagle,
                        hawk,
I have been too attentive
            to the gaudiest birds.

Cafe talk adorns,
              or scorns.
We agree upon
      the language of locusts
          and a salutary
              coursing
                  unhappiness.
What sign
      what visitation
          can delay
the nibbling insistence,
the resigned decay,
all those tatters and terebinths
          we think necessary?
Love invents our bodies' devices,
moment to moment, or
          instant to eternity,
begins the fragmentary
          construction
that speaks of unacknowledged
                          loss.
I have seen doves
pecking at olives on a plate.

For threepence
she wears a vowel
              that suits her.
That gold indignity,
a floral violation
that has surfaced late
becomes
              nothing of substance.
We speak of wearing
clothes, the ordinary
fit and hue the broken
              body requires.
Do not ask
why the body abandons
its structured bravura
to sit with
              the indecency
that comes speaking
              all too clearly
of a bone-fed density
the flesh disdains.

The aspen sweet
       choir of proposals
               leaves la rue
                       intact.
But what of the brackish
       order
               that slips
away (the mentor proposes)
from the proposed?
Would this be music?
       Would this be a moment's
       rest in the music?
Or a palette of propositions,
a strictly proven
       enharmonic set
that holds the road,
where a stony cottage
       dreams of a fugitive—
(say no now to the inadmissible)
and here I will begin again
with my sweet aspen choir.

There is a pentatonic
exasperation
            in choirless birds,
a desire to undermine
the nobility of country states,
or to sit silent
at the day's descent
            into
the cantica minora
      of corrupted light.

I have heard that willows
clarify a lake
        and propose
a depth of justice
   in the surrounding earth.
Only they, perhaps,
will contest the majesty
      of water, or argue
with its changing form.
Remind me of the benevolent
expense of hidden dangers,
of the argument of rivers,
     modulating
       into
the dissonant affection
      of praise.

Whatever at this depth
appears invincible in water
water enfolds,
                and the spare
treasures of coral entanglements
answer the question
the electric fish have put
            to a solar intrusion.
Let the mayfly
        skim the surface
            of its own illusion,
and the croakers go bust
in a barrel of muddy fleece.
These are the sovereignties
oceans never know,
                and I
await their containment.

Now come back to the word
charged with proprietary schemes,
        a lustig locale
of available difference,
the ἱερο-χθων of ambiguity.
Who could wish
        for the purple
                indifference of prophets?

The bone's obliquity
        is a slow growth.
        The eye will never see
        it; the spirit will give it
room and celebrate
        its triumph;
the mind will deny you
the right
        to speak
        of its betrayal.

These days go,
          one by one,
beyond
          the simplicity of rising
and lying down.
          That assertive red astilbe
          seems comfortable with
the blue lady's greeny indulgence,
the white hydrangea's benevolence.
Perhaps I can make sense
of a dry earth, or an acid
that draws beauty from the soil.
Such precision will comfort
the indigo bunting,
                    asleep
in a darkening forest
                    of lilacs.

The first parable of a black
marble unwinds
      where the wind lies
threadbare and consonant
      with old loam.
You must insist
      on gratitude,
the coltish beatitude
we could attribute
      to angels.
But these markers prohibit
the syntax of injury,
      perhaps the clarity
forsaken by a pebble
growing glacial
      under
      a most
intimate pressure,
and speak no way
of the negative armor
      of black.

Chipichipi. The wet intention of day,
                    a changing light.
Veracruz sits this morning
in the safety of mariscos, pan dulce,
                    well-bred coffee.
La loca on the bench repeats her story,
or the story space has given her.
Why not sit with la loca,
and watch the city move from east to west?
Oh, what a clever dance of flowers
this danzón records.
And the spell of attention
required to assess the moment
when the thunder insists
                    upon its rights
in the hummingbird's wings
seems an investment
                    in a cloud.
I was delighted
        when the virgin
honored me with passionflower pollen,
and thought,
waywardly, of the long-flowered

four o'clock, springing to life at dusk.
So what, if the dark brings
        only the memory of the doublestar
and the recognition of a home
                troubled by my absence?
I call your attention now
to the formal intention of a spider,
weaving a cradle for the rose-haired light.

FIVE / KÚMÚ

Who would envision
      the counter fugue
        of twilight,
or the incidental music
    that comes when death
      sounds its leading tone?
No iambic figure
      stirs the worship of absence,
but you will hear
     the melismatic advance
       of the perfect solitude.

Now night is all.
Streams of equivalent temper
sound in the distance. One must trust
that substance, the disputation
of falling measures. You might hear
the peristaltic flow of the wood,
the tunneling speech of heavy
birds, the tense capitulation
in the arbor's disrupted lift.
There is no need for the special
light, the indubitable power
that has learned to count the hours
from grammar to grammar and back
again, when under its own weight,
it begins to dance. What would you now think
of the exorbitant syntax of stars
who coddle their silence? You know I know
the confusion of singular
bodies, the unadorned sequence
a demonstrative soul will set spinning.
I tie you to the adequate
measure of night, to the flighty
day, to love's formal evasion,
the capable, shaping water
of intelligible absence.
                    If night is all.

Speak carefully of the living
and cautiously of the dead.
Don Jorge loves cemeteries,
and deplores the ice in Boston.
You think you can do away
with the fish smell in Veracruz,
or that you have the coffee
under control on Madero;
                    why bother about
these Cambridge exigencies,
the prunish abilities
it takes to treat
                    with an exuberant
                                        world?
Uruguayos have my number.
I have been accused
of translating Corrientes
                    into a milonga
that no one can sing,
                    suffer,
                    or understand,
and few know the batuque
I have written for my grave.

Seamus knew the shape
of an absolute past.
Think of that Aramaic word,
sitting like a siskin
                    in early snow.
God forgive the man
his arrogance, his blasphemy,
        or his anxiety.
What should he show,
if not the endless
        opening of fields,
where his presence
was an offense to other
birds sitting at Vespers?
One hears
the version of an Egyptian
secretary,
who, borrowing the black
and white inscription
        of a desert domain,
felt the bone order,
the logical fragility of a
                    caterpillar
in an abandoned garden.

How clever must the voice be
to sustain a grief
            nurtured
by the exuberant
            descent of a summer morning?

Arché and augury,
		the flux in despair
			the feverish iconology
that awakens death,
argue against a blessing.
I have learned
		the turbulence of names,
the impurity that compels
		that surrounding fiction.
Ah, but now go tell,
		if you may and if you might,
what a spring of ambrosial
verses you might find
			as a guest
				wherever
					joy is raised.

The barberry bush might welcome
the vertiginous coursing
of winter,
and the sedum autumn joy,
cocooned in its russet coat,
might feel delight
in the vagrancies
of deepest January,
but the frangible body of autumn
has removed all evidence,
and marked a tempered threnos
with an unrequited
ecstasy.

Mid-June
the dogwood comes in disguise,
its white beard shaved,
the auroral bathing
                    now done
only by reticular surmise.
How is that possible,
if nothing the catbird
stirs in the morning's crucible,
fissiparous, diminished by thirds,
awakens a hunger
                    for awakenings,
the mistaken flavor
of misplaced thunder?
Quick as the cleft foot
          the leaf will color.

The Szechuan motion of lemons,
no dancing measure certainly,
still sets me aglow,

                a pace
a riveting notion
        that borrows its grace
                from an ancient seed.
There is no need
for the ambiguous invasion
        the surly aspens mount
                against the wind.
The world arises in forgetfulness:
and there I have rewritten
the exhilarating text of one
        who had strayed
from the sullen brown of his
                appleless plane,
unaware of the Szechuan
        motion of lemons.

My imaginary number
sits with the cuckoo at sunset.
Who has dressed it
for such flagrant display?
Such gilded assertiveness
belongs in the bedrock of mines,
and the voice you hear
should be a cricketing carol
redolent of snapping leaves.
But leave this banker where
you found him, sheltered
by omissions, lacunae,
the linear tremor of a real presence,
the smoke of hypothesis.
No one will dispute
          the harmony emptiness brings.

Perhaps the Lord at the Time of Dawn
prepares this shifting domain.
One by one,
        those who constantly
                miss the mark
awaken to a silence
each morning
                suborns.
Need now knows no
thorough intention, no
replenishment
        of unmarked light.

The red that embraces
        the hummingbird trumpet
            set near this stream
appears the color of sunset
                at Montevideo,
a shady phenomenon,
or a confusion that opens
the heart to its tangled presence.
        One must believe
in the slender pod of existence
that speaks
        softly
            to the blessed
bereavement of bones.

You come to the end of the stream
at the point of a slippery rock
where the frog sits
                        in its stillness.
Speak of shame.
What does it care
that you have a need to see
and hear the figurative
        dance of the Poire,
or that you have
        wandered from
the curl of a magnetic field?
Oh, for such eyes.
Oh, for that green voice
                content with silence.

So what would a lady be,
if she were she,
when I began my book?
I deplore
all lions and roses curtained
on a cautious page.
Berry wise I am,
but, focused upon a Python
disencumbrance,
I have forgotten the music.
Who, anyhow,
can sing, when the woman
stands, fully clothed,
                    too close
to the stream,
and the beavers batter
about her feet
                    and call my name?

May fades.
The ostensible clarity of rain
becomes light's impeccable
                    promise.
One will work hard
        to uncover the splendor
            that piping pays,
or that spring of ambrosial
verses at Thebes.
Not for me
        the dithyrambic insistence
                of Sparta,
the Cordoban tolling
set like an epinikion
                of suffering.
Something too iambic
                    enters here.
Some would attribute
this failing to spring's demise
        and summer's impossible
                    delay.
That, we must endeavor to say,
        is the way. The scurrilous

festivity that gives birth
to one who can speak
        of foreign furrows
becomes faith's dispersed
                    relation.
And is the way:
        φέρων μέλοσ ἔρχομαι.
Who now bears the song,
if, at the end of the agora,
        the Pythian artificer
            has lain apart
                since his death?
I return to May
    that rhythm freed of rule,
        that austerity in praise.

Canta, rana,
my elemented nature,
speak to me of home,
that traveler's entreaty
        etched·on the bones,
or of the compassionate coursing
of near desert streams,
or of the October air
     that signals ξενία
passing or to come.
I have learned
that there is no Cartesian anxiety
in the ruffed-neck hummingbird,
the quaking aspen
        or the waterlily.
One must go out,
nevertheless,
from that absolute ground
in search of a contradiction,
perhaps a recalcitrance
     of corn stalk
        or shell,
or of the reality of a satisfied

intellect
        that must verify
               its soul.
Cuate,
     da-quia-dedisti,
return me to a water oak
I have never seen,
remove the autumn sheen
of a sumac that burns my eye.
It then must follow
    that somewhere, someone
will attend this downy
exuberance that keeps you
             singing.

I know
　　or I begin
with the mask that makes me
a gregarious alder
or the holly that defends
　　　the clay path to the well
　　　　　　　　　below.
If, so,
I have strewn
a watercourse where none exists,
alabada sea la infinita urdimbre
——the mask that gives birth
　　　　to my becoming.
Deformation becomes me,
　　　a figure upon a vase,
　　　　　an instrument without
　　　　　　　　measure,
or say, indeed, that my
khorodidaskolos has tuned the act
that perfectly reveals
　　　my tongue-tied ambivalence
when the chorus calls my name.
　　　But sacred days impress me

only in their imperfection,
in the stoked fires
that bear witness to the absent
fig leaves,

       the white lead,
a mask of fine linen,
or in the assertive discrepancy
of my body's presence,

         here,

            now,
where to speak at all
is to enter the light of the bluest

                   star
and the imponderable water
that draws me close

        to the you
          that is I.

How fragile the southern catalpa,
having lost its native syntax.
What would it give
for the ontological form
              in native waters,
or a return to the sun's
devastating constancy?
I have a passion
for the heart-shaped leaves,
the white flowers,
so intense that I have
considered another name
            for its truest being
and a truculent garment
to cover its greyish
                innocence.
In Mali, perhaps,
I would understand this
silence
as the necessary bone,
the possible substance
           of shelter,
and be ready to renew my faith

in an ornamental rosebud.
Call that a savory tree,
so full of legend
and perfect discrepancies,
a ceremonial voice,
a word, if you will,
that compensates for love's
                    disappearance.
I now give you
the synthetic language
of the rose-breasted grosbeak,
the ruffed grouse,
the swallow-tailed kite,
the creative act
          that never began
and dares you to conceive
                    its end.

A book like this
grows from twigs and incense,
the kinds of things you can buy
in bunches,
                    and never understand.
Its lines get tangled
in the transumptive misdirection
        of bird calls,
            a widow's dance,
Neptune's adobe presence
and the Scorpion insistence
        of a father's absent prayers.
Perhaps it lives only in its
            deciduous ambiguity.
            Leave it here—
a rock, or turtle shell,
        disguised by the sun.

Petros Abatzoglou, *What Does Mrs. Freeman Want?*

Pierre Albert-Birot, *Grabinoulor*

Yuz Aleshkovsky, *Kangaroo*

Felipe Alfau, *Chromos* ▪ *Locos*

Ivan Ângelo, *The Celebration* ▪ *The Tower of Glass*

David Antin, *Talking*

António Lobo Antunes, *Knowledge of Hell*

Alain Arias-Misson, *Theatre of Incest*

Djuna Barnes, *Ladies Almanack* ▪ *Ryder*

John Barth, *LETTERS* ▪ *Sabbatical*

Donald Barthelme, *The King* ▪ *Paradise*

Svetislav Basara, *Chinese Letter*

Mark Binelli, *Sacco and Vanzetti Must Die!*

Andrei Bitov, *Pushkin House*

Louis Paul Boon, *Chapel Road* ▪ *Summer in Termuren*

Roger Boylan, *Killoyle*

Ignácio de Loyola Brandão, *Teeth under the Sun* ▪ *Zero*

Bonnie Bremser, *Troia: Mexican Memoirs*

Christine Brooke-Rose, *Amalgamemnon*

Brigid Brophy, *In Transit*

Meredith Brosnan, *Mr. Dynamite*

Gerald L. Bruns, *Modern Poetry and the Idea of Language*

Evgeny Bunimovich and J. Kates, eds., *Contemporary Russian Poetry: An Anthology*

Gabrielle Burton, *Heartbreak Hotel*

Michel Butor, *Degrees* ▪ *Mobile* ▪ *Portrait of the Artist as a Young Ape*

G. Cabrera Infante, *Infante's Inferno* ▪ *Three Trapped Tigers*

Julieta Campos, *The Fear of Losing Eurydice*

Anne Carson, *Eros the Bittersweet*

Camilo José Cela, *Christ versus Arizona* ▪ *The Family of Pascual Duarte* ▪ *The Hive*

Louis-Ferdinand Céline, *Castle to Castle* ▪ *Conversations with Professor Y* ▪ *London Bridge* ▪ *North* ▪ *Rigadoon*

Hugo Charteris, *The Tide Is Right*

Jerome Charyn, *The Tar Baby*

Marc Cholodenko, *Mordechai Schamz*

Emily Holmes Coleman, *The Shutter of Snow*

Robert Coover, *A Night at the Movies*

Stanley Crawford, *Some Instructions to My Wife*

Robert Creeley, *Collected Prose*

René Crevel, *Putting My Foot in It*

Ralph Cusack, *Cadenza*

Susan Daitch, *L.C.* ▪ *Storytown*

Nicholas Delbanco, *The Count of Concord*

Nigel Dennis, *Cards of Identity*

Peter Dimock, *A Short Rhetoric for Leaving the Family*

Ariel Dorfman, *Konfidenz*

Coleman Dowell, *The Houses of Children* ▪ *Island People* ▪ *Too Much Flesh and Jabez*

Rikki Ducornet, *The Complete Butcher's Tales* ▪ *The Fountains of Neptune* ▪ *The Jade Cabinet* ▪ *Phosphor in Dreamland* ▪ *The Stain* ▪ *The Word "Desire."*

William Eastlake, *The Bamboo Bed* ▪ *Castle Keep* ▪ *Lyric of the Circle Heart*

Jean Echenoz, *Chopin's Move*

Stanley Elkin, *A Bad Man* ▪ *Boswell: A Modern Comedy* ▪ *Criers and Kibitzers, Kibitzers and Criers* ▪ *The Dick Gibson Show* ▪ *The Franchiser* ▪ *George Mills* ▪ *The Living End* ▪ *The MacGuffin* ▪ *The Magic Kingdom* ▪ *Mrs. Ted Bliss* ▪ *The Rabbi of Lud* ▪ *Van Gogh's Room at Arles*

Annie Ernaux, *Cleaned Out*

Lauren Fairbanks, *Muzzle Thyself* ▪ *Sister Carrie*

Leslie A. Fiedler, *Love and Death in the American Novel*

Gustave Flaubert, *Bouvard and Pécuchet*

Ford Madox Ford, *The March of Literature*

Jon Fosse, *Melancholy*

Max Frisch, *I'm Not Stiller* ▪ *Man in the Holocene*

Carlos Fuentes, *Christopher Unborn* ▪ *Distant Relations* ▪ *Terra Nostra* ▪ *Where the Air Is Clear*

Janice Galloway, *Foreign Parts* ▪ *The Trick Is to Keep Breathing*

FOR A FULL LIST OF PUBLICATIONS,

VISIT: WWW.DALKEYARCHIVE.COM